INSECTS

SEYMOUR SIMON

HARPER

An Imprint of HarperCollins*Publishers*

This book is lovingly dedicated to Liz Nealon,
my wife, companion, and helpmate.

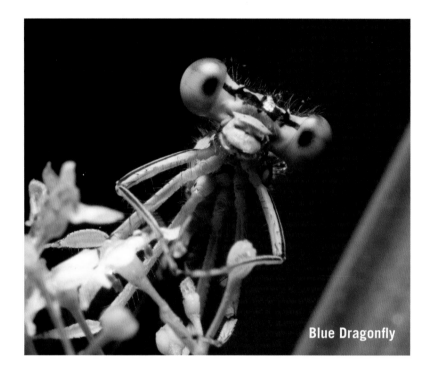

Blue Dragonfly

PHOTO CREDITS

Page 2: © Kletr/Shutterstock; pages 4–5: © Steve Byland/Shutterstock; page 7: © Branko Jovanovic/Shutterstock; page 8: © WathanyuSowong/Shutterstock; page 9: © reptiles4all/Shutterstock; page 10: © QiuJu Song/Shutterstock; page 11: © Palo_ok/ Shutterstock; page 12: © nico99/Shutterstock; page 13: © Ratchapol Yindeesuk/Shutterstock; page 15: © D. Kucharski K. Kucharska/Shutterstock; page 16: © MarcelClemens/Shutterstock; page 19: © Aksenova Natalya/Shutterstock; page 20: © Ling Kuok Loung/Shutterstock; page 21: © Alex Hyde/naturepl.com.; page 23: © Miroslav Hlavko/Shutterstock; page 24: © enciktat/ Shutterstock; page 26: © Daniel Prudek/Shutterstock; page 27: © schankz/Shutterstock; page 28: © BGS_Image/Shutterstock; page 29: © Peter Waters/Shutterstock; page 31: © aslysun/Shutterstock; page 32: © Paul Reeves Photography/Shutterstock; page 33, top to bottom: © Bildagentur Zoonar GmbH/Shutterstock; © Radu Bercan/Shutterstock; page 34: © Liew Weng Keong/Shutterstock; page 35: © juniors/juniors/Superstock; page 36: © Christian Musat/Shutterstock; pages 38–39: © JLBarranco/Getty Images (US), Inc.

Library of Congress Control Number: 2015938991
ISBN 978-0-06-228915-5 (trade bdg.) — ISBN 978-0-06-228914-8 (pbk.)

16 17 18 19 20 SCP 10 9 8 7 6 5 4 3 2 1

❖

First Edition

Author's Note

From a young age, I was interested in animals, space, my surroundings—all the natural sciences. When I was a teenager, I became the president of a nationwide junior astronomy club with a thousand members. After college, I became a classroom teacher for nearly twenty-five years while also writing articles and books for children on science and nature even before I became a full-time writer. My experience as a teacher gives me the ability to understand how to reach my young readers and get them interested in the world around us.

I've written more than 250 books, and I've thought a lot about different ways to encourage interest in the natural world, as well as how to show the joys of nonfiction. When I write, I use comparisons to help explain unfamiliar ideas, complex concepts, and impossibly large numbers. I try to engage your senses and imagination to set the scene and to make science fun. For example, in *Penguins*, I emphasize the playful nature of these creatures on the very first page by mentioning how penguins excel at swimming and diving. I use strong verbs to enhance understanding. I make use of descriptive detail and ask questions that anticipate what you may be thinking (sometimes right at the start of the book).

Many of my books are photo-essays, which use extraordinary photographs to amplify and expand the text, creating different and engaging ways of exploring nonfiction. You'll also find a glossary, an index, and website and research recommendations in most of my books, which make them ideal for enhancing your reading and learning experience. As William Blake wrote in his poem, I want my readers "to see a world in a grain of sand, / And a heaven in a wild flower, / Hold infinity in the palm of your hand, / And eternity in an hour."

Seymour Simon

Cicada

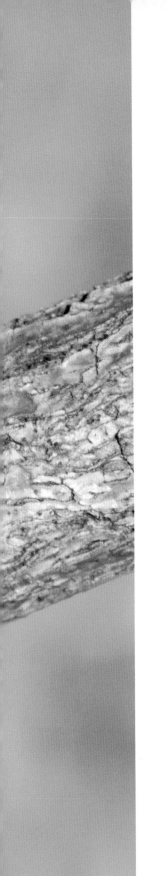

Many people call any insect they see a bug. That's fine, even though it's not exactly scientific. All bugs are insects, but not all insects are bugs. It's as if you were calling all **mammals** cats. It's true that all cats are mammals, but not all mammals are cats. There are many other kinds of mammals that are not cats, such as dogs, elephants, whales, and even people.

According to scientists, bugs are only one group of insects. Scientists divide all insects into about twenty-five different groups called orders. Bugs are insects that belong to an order called Hemiptera, which means "half wing" in Greek. They get this name because their front wings look like a half wing. Scientists call the insects in that order "true bugs." All true bugs have half wings and sucking mouthparts.

You can still call insects any name you want to, though. You can call them "creepy crawlies," "insects," or "bugs." But now you know why a scientist might correct you if he or she hears you use the word "bugs" to mean all insects.

All insects are *invertebrates*, animals that do not have a backbone. They do not have an internal skeleton the way we and other animals such as dogs, cats, birds, snakes, and frogs do. Instead, insects have a hard shell on the outside of their bodies called an *exoskeleton*. Insects belong to a group of invertebrates that have jointed legs and are called *arthropods*.

Not all arthropods are insects. You can be sure an arthropod is an insect if it has six legs and a body with three sections—a head, a thorax (in the middle), and an abdomen (stomach). Insects also have two antennae (feelers) coming from their heads, and they hatch from eggs. Most kinds of insects have either one or two pairs of wings. That's why ants, bees, grasshoppers, and dragonflies are insects. They are all arthropods with six legs, three body parts, and two antennae, and they hatch from eggs.

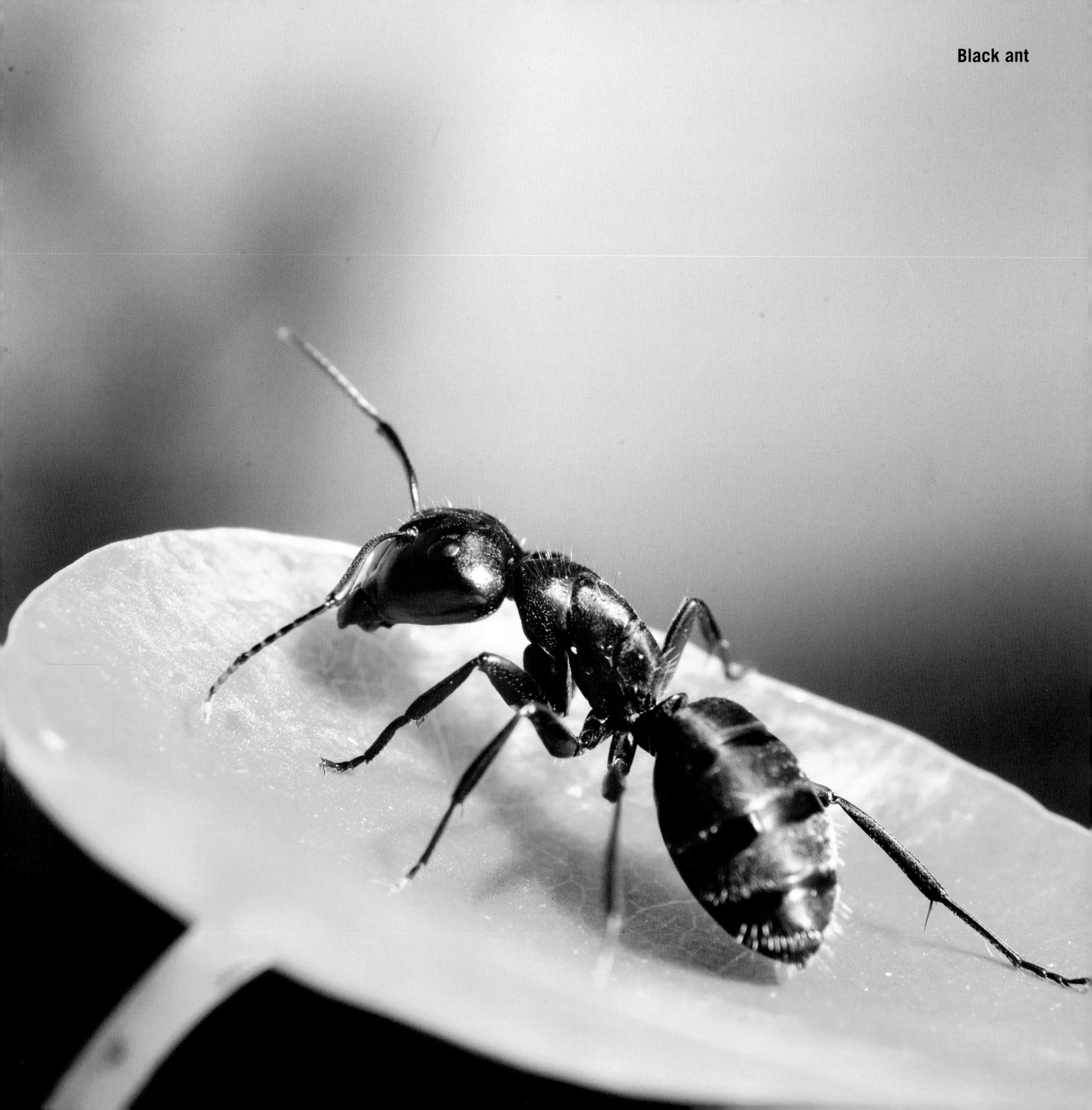
Black ant

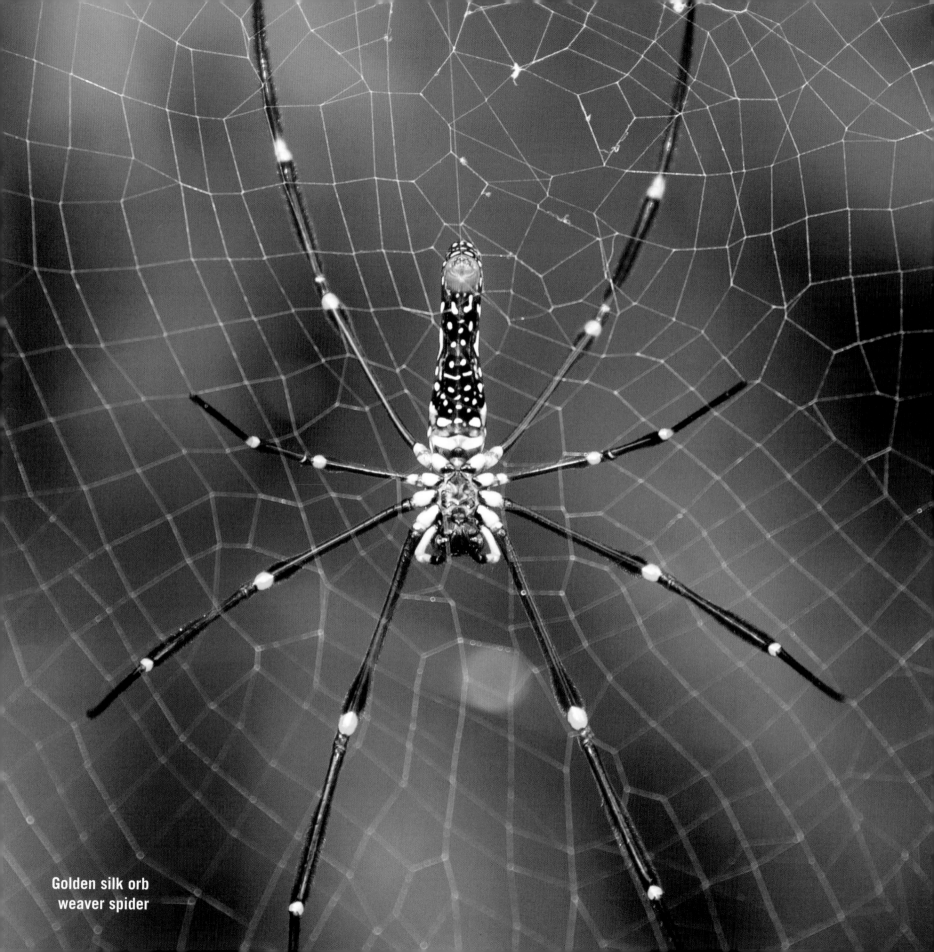

Golden silk orb
weaver spider

Spiders are often mistaken for insects, but they are not. Spiders have eight legs rather than six legs. Unlike insects, their bodies have only two parts—the head and the abdomen. They don't have antennae or wings.

There are also many other small creepy crawlers, such as centipedes and millipedes, that are not insects because they don't have the right number of legs or body parts.

Indian giant
tiger centipede

Baby animals such as kittens and puppies look pretty much the same as they grow into adults. They just grow bigger. But many insects change shape and look completely different as they grow. The change that insects go through is called **metamorphosis**. Metamorphosis for ants, bees, beetles, butterflies, and other insects has four stages: egg, larva, pupa, and adult.

Insects begin as eggs. The eggs hatch into a soft, worm-like shape called a larva. You have seen a larva if you've ever seen a caterpillar, which is the

Asian ladybird larvae

Caterpillar

larval stage of a butterfly. Larvae are big eaters. They can eat several times their own weight every day. If a human baby grew as fast as an insect larva, he or she would grow into a giant!

Larvae often run out of space to grow because their skins don't expand. So from time to time they shed their skins. The old skin splits open and the larval insect climbs out. The new skin quickly begins to harden. At the end of the larva stage, the insect makes a hard body covering called a pupa. The insect lives inside the pupa and changes shape completely. Once it leaves the pupa, an insect is a fully grown adult. A few insects, such as grasshoppers and crickets, go through an incomplete metamorphosis. They hatch from eggs and just grow bigger as they shed their old skins and grow new ones.

Praying mantis

There are at least four times more kinds of insects than all other kinds of animals combined. Scientists have already counted nearly a million different kinds of insects and think that there are millions more still to be discovered.

Some insects are as small as the period at the end of this sentence. Other kinds of insects are two or three inches long. There are insects with thin, long pencil-shaped bodies, and other insects with round ball-shaped bodies. There are insects that you may have seen often, such as ants, bees, and butterflies. Other insects are rarely seen and look like creatures from distant worlds.

Spiny leaf insect

Scientists think that the numbers of individual insects alive at any one time today is about 10 quintillion (that's 10 followed by 18 zeros). That means that there are about 200 million insects for every human on Earth. To put it another way, for every pound of a living human being, there are several hundred pounds of living insects.

Why are there so many different kinds of insects? Scientists think that these great numbers are the results of insects' small size, their ability to live in many different kinds of environments, the fact that they can fly, and their long history on Earth.

Firebugs

Dragonfly fossil

If you could travel back to the time of the dinosaurs, and even before that, you would see that insects existed hundreds of millions of years ago. We know that because they left behind **fossils**, imprints of themselves in the rock. Many of these early insects were giants, much greater in size than their modern **descendants**. There were cockroaches as big as cats and dragonflies as big as eagles. Why did these truly giant insects **vanish** and why do they no longer exist?

Some scientists believe that in dinosaur times, there was much more oxygen in Earth's atmosphere. Oxygen is the gas that most animals, including insects, need to breathe in order to live. In **prehistoric** times, insects and other animals breathed air that contained much more oxygen than the air does today. The additional oxygen reached much deeper into an insect's body to feed its cells. That meant that an insect's body could be several feet long, much bigger than it can be with oxygen in the air nowadays.

As the amount of oxygen decreased in the atmosphere over millions of years, the giant insects died off. Smaller insects survive better with less oxygen, and so insects changed over time into the kinds that live now.

Insects have eyes and can see light but not the same way we do. Insects see the world around them very differently than people or animals like dogs and cats. Humans and most other larger animals have eyes with a single lens. But insects have eyes that are made up of many tiny lenses, called compound eyes. Some insects, such as flies, bees, and dragonflies, have hundreds of tiny lenses in each eye. So many lenses mean that insect vision is much different than ours.

But exactly what insects see is not easy for us to know or find out. Does each lens record just a tiny part of their view so that they see a whole assortment of tiny views that make up an object? To us, that might look as if we were looking through one end of a bunch of soda straws, but we have no idea what those images viewed by an insect look like to them.

We do know that insects see colors differently than we do. Insects don't see yellow, orange, and red colors very well. They do see blue and violet and even **ultraviolet**, which we cannot see. That's why we use yellow or red lightbulbs so as not to attract insects at night, or even to study them without them knowing we're watching. We also use ultraviolet light to attract night-flying insects into traps, or bug zappers. But why moths and other night insects are attracted to lights at all is a question scientists have not yet answered.

Compound eyes of a common horsefly

For most insects, sight is a lot less important than the senses of smell, touch, and hearing. Many insects have a sense of smell that is incredible compared to a human's sense of smell. Different insects use their sense of smell to find food, avoid enemies, find their way to their nests, find a mate, and even communicate with each other.

Ants as well as many other insects smell with their antennae. On their way out of a colony nest to search for food, ants lay down a chemical trail that is followed by other ants in the colony. Ants can smell food through a layer of earth and even through some kinds of food packaging that we use. Ants constantly touch each other in passing, so that every ant has a common colony odor that identifies it and prevents it from being attacked by other ants in the colony.

Black ant

Male moths use their feathery antennae to sense special smells called **pheromones** (FAIR-uh-moans), which attract them to female moths. For example, one kind of female

Indian luna moth

moth gives off a pheromone so powerful that it attracts male moths from miles away. Attracting pheromones are given off by many other kinds of insects, such as bees and beetles.

Just as insects don't have noses to smell with, they don't have ears on their heads to hear with. Some insects, such as crickets and grasshoppers, hear with "ears" on their legs and stomachs, or they just use antennae to pick up sounds.

Let's learn more about some of the most common insects.

All beetles belong to an insect order called Coleoptera. Beetles make up about 40 percent of all insects. Beetles live everywhere, from land to freshwater lakes and ponds, from deserts to rainforests, from seashore to mountaintops. Even lonely islands in the middle of the oceans have plenty of beetles. Beetles range in size from tiny to very large. The smallest beetle, called the fringed ant beetle, is a tiny speck, smaller than this period. The titan beetle is the biggest known beetle. It can grow to seven inches long and has jaws so strong that it can snap a wooden pencil in half.

Here's what makes an insect a beetle:

- All adult beetles have chewing mouthparts, and they chew their food before swallowing. Most beetles feed on plants but some eat smaller insects, and others feed on **decaying** animal materials.

- Most beetles have tough half wings that protect the more delicate flight wings underneath. When beetles fly, the wing covers are held out to the sides, allowing the flight wings to move freely.

- Beetles complete metamorphosis. The larvae look very different from the adults.

Stag beetle

Cricket

Grasshoppers, crickets, and katydids belong to an order of insects called Orthoptera. The name comes from the Greek words meaning "straight" and "winged." Many insects in this order, such as crickets, make a kind of chirping sound by rubbing their wings together or against their legs. They can hear the sound with "ears" located on their legs or on their abdomens. All the insects in the order Orthoptera

- have leathery wings that are folded and flattened back against their bodies when not flying;

- look very much alike as young insects and as adults;

- have chewing mouthparts;

- are usually very large compared to other kinds of insects;

- have antennae that are big and easy to spot.

Honeybee

Bees and wasps belong to an order of insects called Hymenoptera. Their name comes from the Greek words meaning "membrane" and "winged." Ants are also in this same order, but most ants are wingless. Only the queen and the reproducing male ants have wings; the workers in ant colonies have no wings.

Scientists say that as much as one third of the food we eat are crops pollinated by bees. But bee colonies have been mysteriously dying off in recent years, and no one is sure of the cause. It is a problem scientists will have to solve soon, or it will negatively affect our food supply.

The insects in this order are alike in these ways:

- Bees and wasps have gauzy wings that you can see through. The front wings are bigger than the back wings.

- Many of the insects in this order, such as ants, live in large groups called colonies.

- The young look like tiny worms or grubs.

- The adult females have stingers.

- They have chewing and sucking mouthparts.

- The middle of their bodies look pinched together.

Wasps

Blue pansy butterfly

Butterflies and moths belong to an order of insects called Lepidoptera. The name comes from the Greek words meaning "scales" and "wings." Scales are the flattened hairs that cover the body and wings of most butterflies and moths. This is the second largest order of insects. There are more than eleven thousand different kinds of butterflies and moths known.

The larvae are usually called caterpillars. Caterpillars have a head with chewing mouthparts, and they eat leaves, stems, and roots. Adult butterflies and moths have large wings (compared to their body size) that are covered by tiny scales. The scales often reflect light in beautiful colored patterns on the wings.

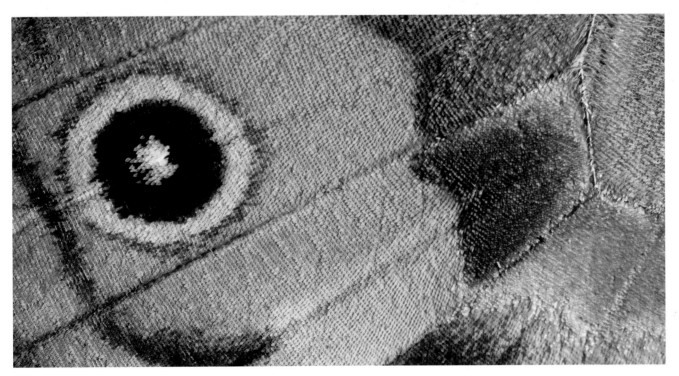

Close-up of common brown butterfly wing

Butterflies and moths are similar in these ways:

- The adults have two pairs of large wings. Larvae (caterpillars) are wingless.

- Most adults have sucking mouthparts. Some have no mouthparts at all and only live long enough to mate before they die.

- Larvae have chewing mouthparts.

- Butterflies have antennae with knobs on their ends. Moths have feathery antennae.

- Larvae form cocoons during the pupa stage before they emerge as adults.

Butterfly emerges from chrysalis.

Twelve-spotted skimmer dragonfly

Dragonflies and damselflies belong to an order called Odonata. The word comes from a Greek word meaning "tooth." It refers to the strong teeth found in the jaws of most adults in this order. Both the young and adults in this order **prey** on other animals for food. The adults are great fliers that feed on mosquitoes and gnats. The young live in water and eat anything they can find, including small fishes and tadpoles.

Azure damselfly

Dragonflies and damselflies are similar in these ways:

- They have large, beautiful pairs of wings with patterns. When they're flying or at rest, dragonflies' wings are extended outward like an airplane. Damselfly wings are folded together when at rest.
- They have long, thin bodies with no stingers. (Dragonflies can bite though!)
- They have short antennae.
- They have very large eyes in **proportion** to their heads.
- The young, called nymphs, live in water.

Flies belong to the order Diptera. The name comes from the Greek words meaning "two" and "wings." Their second pair of wings is very small. Flies are quick to take off and **maneuver** in air.

Housefly

There are so many insects that just listing each kind would take thousands upon thousands of book pages. Here are some other interesting insects that you might like to know about:

Giraffe weevil

- The many kinds of treehoppers are the strangest-looking insects. They look like thorns growing on branches rather than insects. Also competing for the strangest looking are giraffe weevils and violin beetles.

- Butterflies and moths are the most beautiful kinds of insects. Particularly beautiful are luna moths, birdwing butterflies, and sunset moths.

- Dragonflies are the fastest insects on the wing. Some zip along at 35 miles per hour, much faster than you can run at top speed. Hawk moths are nearly as fast as dragonflies.

- The goliath beetle from Africa is the heaviest insect, weighing nearly a quarter of a pound, about the weight of a good-sized hamburger.

- The giant stick insect is the longest insect. When it stretches out its legs, it measures about a foot and a half.

- The feather-winged beetle and the fairy moth are the smallest insects, both of which are smaller than this period.

Goliath beetle

Many different kinds of insects are helpful to humans. Some kinds, ladybugs and praying mantises for example, are helpful because they feed on insects that eat crops such as vegetables and flowers.

Even more important for people are the insects that pollinate plants. You may have seen bees, wasps, and butterflies visiting flowers. Flowers have sweet nectar that many insects feed upon. When insects visit flowers to feed, they accidentally pick up pollen on their feet or their bodies. As they visit other flowers, insects drop the pollen and pick up more. When pollen from one flower lands on another flower, seeds are formed. Without insects that pollinate crops and wildflowers, we would have far fewer crops to feed people, and many kinds of plants would not survive.

Insects can be harmful to people as well. Some kinds of insects, such as locusts, eat crops in huge amounts. Huge swarms of locusts may sweep across farmlands and strip away all the plants down to bare earth. This can lead to starvation in the lands affected. Other kinds of insects, such as wasps, hornets, and killer bees, have stings that are very painful and, in rare cases, can even cause death.

There is no doubt, though, that insects benefit people more than they harm them. Pollination by insects alone is essential for many plants we rely upon. Many scientists believe that without the activities of insects, human life on our planet could not exist.

Insects live their lives doing the things necessary for them to survive. There are so many different kinds of insects that we know about, and there may be millions more that we have yet to discover.

Insects are easy to study; you don't have to go far to find an insect to watch. But we could study insects all our lives and not learn all there is to know about them. Insects may be small, but their presence in the world is huge and they're exciting to learn about.

GLOSSARY

Decaying—When natural processes cause something to rot.

Descendant—A person, animal, or insect that originated from an earlier form of that person, animal, or insect.

Fossils—The remains or impressions of a once-living thing.

Mammal—A type of animal that usually has fur or hair covering its skin.

Maneuver—A planned or skillful movement or action.

Metamorphosis—The change that insects go through in their lives that consists of four stages: egg, larva, pupa, and adult.

Pheromone—A powerful chemical an animal or insect releases to attract or influence the behavior of another animal or insect of the same species.

Prehistoric—Relating to a period or the time before history was recorded.

Prey—An animal that's hunted or captured for food.

Proportion—A part of the whole.

Ultraviolet—Rays of visible light that are on the violet end of the spectrum.

Vanish—To disappear or stop existing.

INDEX

Bold type indicates illustrations.